I0486767

How NOT to Implement Six Sigma

How NOT to Implement Six Sigma

A manager's guide to ensuring the failure of
the world's greatest Quality Improvement
and Waste Reducing machine.

Norm Friberg and Elaine Kowansky, GELRAD

Copyright © 2006 by Norm Friberg and Elaine Kowansky, GELRAD.
Illustrations by Tanya and Amanda Kraemer

Library of Congress Control Number: 2006902555
ISBN :   Hardcover   1-4257-1227-4
                    Softcover   1-4257-1226-6

All rights reserved. No part of this book may be reproduced or transmitted in any
form or by any means, electronic or mechanical, including photocopying, recording,
or by any information storage and retrieval system, without permission in writing
from the copyright owner.

This book was printed in the United States of America.

To order additional copies of this book, contact:
Xlibris Corporation
1-888-795-4274
www.Xlibris.com
Orders@Xlibris.com
33950

Contents

Note to Reader

Let us start by saying that the authors are ardent and committed proponents of the Six Sigma methodology. We really don't want to see Six Sigma fail in your or any other organization. We believe that Six Sigma, done right, is the best, most reliable approach to quality improvement, customer satisfaction excellence, and cost savings available today.

Further, we do not really believe that a whole underground of corporate saboteurs are buying this book to use as a handbook for their nefarious activities. Such people do exist, but they already have their agendas. No, we have written this book to help you, the committed Six Sigma Champion, to identify the kinds of actions that can seriously jeopardize your efforts, though they may be committed unintentionally, or even with the best of intentions.

We hope you enjoy some of our attempts at humor, and maybe have a chuckle or two as you read the following pages. Keep in mind however that the concerns are real, and, although our negative-thinking manager may or may not actually exist, the errors of commission and omission, the gaffes and oversights, can and will happen unless you and your team exercise vigilance and judgment.

N. Friberg and E. Kowansky

Introduction

Okay, so some big-thinking, visionary "Leader" in your company has decided that you need to implement this thing called Six Sigma. He (or she) claims that this latest flavor-of-the-month will cure everything that's wrong with your company overnight and save billions while you're at it. He (or she) points out how companies like General Electric and Ford have attributed billions of dollars in savings to this gimmick over the last few years.

Your problem is: how can you get through the next few months or (God forbid) years until this Six Sigma nonsense blows over?

Worry no more! This book will give you the knowledge, tools, and insights you need to *guarantee* the failure of Six Sigma in your organization. I know this is a big claim, but believe us, many companies have tested and proven these can't-miss ideas. Just follow along with our recommendations and Six Sigma will be out of your hair as quick as a cordless bungee jumper.

How can our methods be so effective, you ask? How can we make this outrageous guarantee? *Because we have seen the results with our own eyes!* Smart, no-nonsense managers in many companies, large and small, successful and otherwise, have found these methods effective every time—and it doesn't take a big-bucks consultant to make it happen. You can implement these super six-sigma-busting actions from the comfort and privacy of your corner office. No high-cost computer software is required. All you need is your telephone (e-mail is optional) and your personal authority to make it happen.

So relax, Mr. (or Ms.) Manager! We guarantee that just a few pages into this book and you will be making decisions that will severely cripple this Six Sigma "thing". After you've finished the book, you'll be laughing out loud watching your dispirited underlings and confused executives running for cover, and denying that they ever wanted Six Sigma in the first place. After that, you'll be able to sit back and smile as they all come crawling back to your office, asking for forgiveness, and pleading with you for the **real solution** to the company's problems (which of course, you already have—you've just been waiting for the right moment to whip it out and be the hero that you deserve to be, right?).

Imagine the freedom, the relief, you will feel when this annoying Six Sigma thing is off your back and the do-gooder, technoid dreamers who thought it up are back writing their resumes. And you CAN do it! Start today!

Chapter 1

The Golden Rule

Everything you read—and I mean everything—about Six Sigma, says that this methodology is a culture-changing innovation for your company. Six Sigma is meant to be integrated into the very business processes and thinking of every division, department, manager and employee. So, given your desire to kill Six Sigma before it can get deeply ingrained, your first mission is to take every possible opportunity to make sure that people think of it as a "flash in the pan".

An easy and fun approach to this is to adopt the following: Whenever anyone mentions "Six Sigma," "Black Belts" or "Breakthrough," Simply give a sly, knowing grin, and roll your eyes, as if to say "yeah, right." If you can manage a little wink to one of your unconverted colleagues, that will help. Try not to be too conspicuous to the Six Sigma leader, as this could be construed as your being something other than a "team player," and you sure don't want that. Just keep it subtle, for now.

Remember, you fully expect, and want, Six Sigma to go away and leave you alone. If you're lucky and have a CEO who's amenable, you can try this trick at a management meeting. When it comes up on the agenda, just look puzzled and say, "Six Sigma? But I thought we already talked about that last time. Didn't we?" Some of your colleagues will get the hint and join right in and agree with you.

A few stubborn adherents to the program may say something like, "You don't understand, Phil, Six Sigma isn't a one-shot deal. It has to be integrated into the day-to-day running of the company."

Now, you don't want to give credibility to these people, so don't argue with them. Instead, be condescending. Say something like, "Oh sure Fred, that's understood. I thought it already was integrated, and since we have such a tight agenda today, I thought we could just move on to the more pressing stuff, like the lunch menu. Why don't we get that squared away so Doris can order from the cafeteria . . ." You get the idea.

If you're really good, you can figure out ways to demean Six Sigma at almost every opportunity. For example, if a colleague comes looking for Joe, just tell them, "Oh, Joe's probably at one of those Six Sigma meetings again. I haven't seen his face since he went for that Green Belt training." You can make this even more effective by adding something like, "Or is it blue belt? Orange belt? Heck, I can't get that stuff straight." This is sure to get a nod of agreement from the colleague, and raise his opinion of you several notches.

Similarly, try to always talk about Six Sigma as a brief, fleeting event rather than a long-term commitment. Take a cue from former president George H. Bush when he talked about "the vision *thing*." This communicated very clearly how he felt about "vision" and how much energy he was willing to invest in it. If you refer to the program as "the Six Sigma *thing*," everyone will know pretty much where you stand on the issue, without your never having to say it right out loud. Similar demeaning ways of referring to Six Sigma are shown in the following chart. Pick the phrase that suits the occasion. Mix and match.

> Phrases sure to kill confidence in Six Sigma:
>
> That Six Sigma "Thing"
> Demonic, I mean, DMAIC
> Sick Sigma
> Sigma Six (A cartoon show. Should register with the parents of small kids)
> This is like what we tried with TQM a few years ago, right?
> ------------- " -------------------- ISO 9000 ------------ " ---------?
> This Six Sigma B____ S____.

Now, that last one is kind of harsh, and may raise negative thoughts about you with the wrong audience. However, a CEO was heard using this exact phrase when he didn't know who was listening. Everyone in the company knew about it within ten minutes. What better way to pull the rug out from under the whole deal?

You may not be lucky enough to have a CEO with that kind of "vision thing," so you will probably have to be more subtle. If your deployment manager questions your commitment to Six Sigma in front of a large group, don't say anything crazy. Go with the flow: "But Bob, you know I'm a thousand percent behind Six Sigma. I even sent Josephine to the Green Belt training last week." Then follow up with a cleverly-worded indication of your underlying feelings: "You won't be needing her any more for that, will you? She has some important work to catch up with now." The implication being that you don't consider Six Sigma to be all that important, get it?

Always insinuate your belief that Six Sigma is a short-term project: the "Flavor of the Month". You know that's the way the big boss feels about it, so why should you feel any different? Talk freely about how much your department could accomplish "if we didn't have all this Six Sigma stuff going on." Ask your subordinates things like "You're not still working on Six Sigma, are you? I thought that was done already." Make them feel uncomfortable to ask your permission to attend team meetings and training sessions. If they are afraid to ask, you don't have to deny them permission, so you don't come off as negative to your peers.

If you have a Black Belt reporting to you, it's even easier to push Six Sigma to its inevitable demise. Call the Black Belt into your office late on a Friday afternoon and ask him or her, "So tell me what is taking so damn long finishing this DMAIC project you're working on? It's already been two weeks! You have other work to get back to."

The underling will most likely say something like, "Sir, there are specific steps to the DMAIC process that must be followed. That's what makes Six Sigma different and special. If you shortcut the process the results will not be as effective."

You need to come right back at him with this: "Oh come on Ted. You know as well as I do what the solution to the problem is. We don't have enough people (or resources, or equipment, or time, or . . .). If headquarters would just give us the five new engineers we asked for, our problem would be solved, and finishing this project would free you up for some real *value-adding* work." Note the subtle implication at the end. Plant the seed in the Black Belt's mind that his Six Sigma work isn't viewed as serious or important. Watch how quickly he begs out of the program! His career is at stake!

If you give credibility to Six Sigma as a permanent part of the corporate culture, you're working *against* its failure. In the following chapters we will give you many more tips of how to assure that Six Sigma will fail miserably. However, always keep the Golden Rule in mind: ***If you treat Six Sigma like a one-shot deal, then that's the way everyone will start to see it.*** Six Sigma will melt away like yesterday's snowstorm in San Diego.

If you're not trying to make Six Sigma fail, the organization needs to understand the long-range nature of the methodology. Six Sigma works when everyone, from CEO on down, understands and is committed to the long haul. Growing the competence and expertise to make Six Sigma work takes time and careful nurturing. People who only push for, and expect, short-term success are setting up the program for failure. Yes, there will be some small victories as the "quick win" projects bear results. Don't let nay-sayers in the company divert the momentum and energy away from the program with demeaning and demoralizing statements like those above. Everyone must know and agree beforehand that Six Sigma is no "flavor-of-the-month." It is, on the contrary, **"the way we do business from now on."** *Get your people thinking in those terms, and you are well on your way to Six Sigma success.*

I don't know about this Six Sigma Guy. All I know is I'm not raising my hand for anything!

Chapter 2

Picking the wrong people to lead your Six Sigma initiative

Okay, so you're stuck: You have committed to your management that you will implement Six Sigma in your company. You have plenty of other things on your plate, and there are no more hours in the day than there were before you got this assignment. So, how are you supposed to get out of this without looking like a complete incompetent?

Well, thankfully, there is one very easy way to make sure Six Sigma fails that requires minimal work from your side; simply turn it over to the wrong people to manage it for you! This can work at any of a number of levels. You can assign the responsibility to any or all of the following, and then pick the wrong people for the jobs:

1. The Deployment Champion
2. The Consultant
3. The Project Champions
4. The Black Belts
5. The Master Black Belts
6. The Financial Analysts

As you can see, there are ample opportunities to assure failure of the program. We will attempt here to give you easy-to-follow guidelines for making a total muck-up of the whole business!

The Deployment Champion

This individual will most likely be held responsible for the success or failure of the entire Six Sigma effort, so here is your best shot. If you are serious about making it a failure, make sure you select a person who you know can't handle it. This person you want can fall into several categories.

First is a middle manager with a track record for over-complicating and micro-managing everything. This type will lack the imagination, and the commitment to change, that are required to make Six Sigma work. This type manager is perfect for the task described in the title of this book (and you don't need to tell him or her that this is your objective). Chances are that he or she will simply "manage" the program to death. There will be countless (and endless) meetings of the involved parties. He will bore everyone with lengthy presentations intended to prove how he has complete control over the process. In most cases, loud snoring during these presentations will convince other managers that Six Sigma is the equivalent of (and as exciting as) taking inventory at an ice-house in Alaska.

He will also make life miserable for the Black Belts, Green Belts, etc. in demanding frequent, burdensome reports (daily, if possible) that will sap their time and energy away from their project work. Further, he will invent elaborate charts and graphs that confuse all involved parties, instead of having a few well-chosen graphics to communicate the status of Six Sigma.

Another good choice for Deployment Champion is the fast-tracking young over-achiever. Believe it or not, this guy or gal is ideal. If you're sharp, you can get this youngster to promise you that Six Sigma will deliver impressive results in half the time originally planned. That guarantees that there will be many corners cut, many shortcuts taken. Perhaps this person will decide that Green Belt training can be shortened from two weeks to three days, for example. Needless to say, these Green Belts will find their heads spinning and will lack even the most basic understanding of what they are supposed to do.

This type will also try to impress you by deciding to get rid of the consultant far earlier than planned, which is more or less equivalent to throwing your children into the deep end of the pool before they have learned the doggie paddle. This guy has his reputation as a go-getter to protect. That means he or she will drive for results above all else while ignoring the basic needs of the people actually doing the work. Further, after a few months of running Six Sigma, chances are that this young rising star will already be angling for their next big promotion, and Six Sigma will be the last thing on his or her mind.

Favorite quote from a fast-tracker: "Why don't we take what we've done already and put a nice Six Sigma ribbon around it?"

Or you could give this job to "Old Joe". We're not being sexist or ageist here; Old Joe could be 35 and a woman. It's the person who somehow has risen to a management position, but is now seen as having reached the pinnacle of his or her potential, and who shows neither the ability nor the desire for any further advancement.

Putting Old Joe in charge of Six Sigma deployment is an expedient for management. It takes a marginally performing person and puts them in a new, highly challenging position with high visibility. HR will love you for it.

Old Joe will take on a "deer in the headlights" look. He or she will be seen walking the halls late after normal working hours, asking directions from the maintenance staff. OJ will keep his or her office door closed, use more than the usual number of vacation days, and may begin giggling at meetings, seemingly without cause. Luckily, your company's medical plan will cover treatment for Joe's condition. It will not cover the disastrous nosedive of Six Sigma that results.

Finally, of course, you can give the job to a complete incompetent. This is a risky approach, however, and can reflect negatively on you. Remember, your objective is to make the program fail, not to end your career.

The Consultant

Here is another great opportunity. Nobody really likes or trusts consultants, who everyone knows are a bunch of money-grabbing con artists who merely want to take your company for all they can before walking off laughing, all the way to the bank, after the program fails. Make life easy for them: pick a group or individual with little or no experience in Six Sigma implementation. When it becomes obvious they are incompetent, you can fire them with a clear conscience and your boss will consider you a hero. More on this in chapter 8.

The Project Champions

These people will most likely be chosen from the management ranks with little or no knowledge of what Six Sigma is supposed to be about. Be sure to select those managers who are already overburdened or producing borderline performance. These folks are so worried about their next performance reviews that having any responsibility for Six Sigma will put them over the edge.

If by accident you select a Project Champion who is committed and worthy, make sure to minimize their importance by telling them something like this: "Don't sweat this Six Sigma thing, George. You don't really need to do anything. Just make believe you are listening when the Black Belt or Green Belt comes crying to you for help. Pat them on the back, assure them of your support, and show them out of your office. If they screw this thing up, nobody's going to hold you responsible." That should give them the confidence they need to ignore Six Sigma for the rest of the year.

By the way, training for Project Champions is optional. The less they know the better.

Above all, avoid making Six Sigma results a part of their individual performance objectives. The last thing you want to do is to attach Six Sigma to their merit increase or bonus calculation. People who have made this error in the past have realized amazing success with the Six Sigma methodology, and that's what you are trying to avoid, remember?

The Black Belts

This one is tricky, as some people who you would least expect to perform in this role might surprise you and take it quite seriously. Your best bets here are to focus on three types: The Techno-Nerds, the Nervous Nellies, and the Lost Souls.

The Techno-Nerds might be your best bet. These are the people who majored in statistics in college. Maybe they went on to get their PhD's. Everyone knows that they are smart, and chances are they will breeze through the challenging Black Belt training, giving the impression that things are going well. Once they have projects assigned to them, they will charge ahead with precise measurement systems, superb statistical analyses, and insightful planned experiments. They will do all of this on their own without bothering to form a project team or getting the cooperation of the process owner. Their utter inability to interact with other human beings will render all this work pointless, as they will be unable to explain any of it or justify the business impact of their conclusions. With any luck at all, line employees who truly understand the process under study will be so turned off that they will refuse to cooperate with the nerd Black Belt. The Black Belt in question will simply shrug it off and say, "Hey, can I help it if these idiots don't understand?"

The Nervous Nellies come next. Don't be confused by the name; they don't have to be female. These are the people who are too insecure and timid even to ask questions during the training, so they will most likely not even understand the principles and statistical tools you need to run a DMAIC project. They will be too afraid to contact sources of information within the company. When they finally build up the nerve to make a phone call, they are relieved when they get the other person's voice mail. They tend to start conversations with the phrase, "I'm really sorry to bother you, but . . .". They are easily intimidated by managers who are reluctant to participate in the project, and they are equally reluctant to keep their manager and project champion informed, lest they be seen as under-performing.

Give the NN the toughest project possible, like "Reduce Customer Complaints by 100%" or "Solve the World Energy Crisis".

If a Nervous Nellie comes to you because they are having trouble getting information from your colleague in Accounting, say something like, "You can't get old Bill Sloane to talk to you? Why, heck, Bill's a pussy cat. Wait till you have to get information from Janet over in Purchasing. She'll *really* give you a hard time." Never encourage the NN by offering to intercede or by giving them pointers on dealing with these people. If they can't make it work by themselves, too bad.

The Lost Soul is the kind of sad sack employee who accepts the Black Belt position because he knows that his past performance is so bad that he's lucky to have a job at all. Human Resources is a good source for this. Just ask your friend in HR if there are any borderline employees who already have one foot out the door. Your HR friend will say, "Gee, thanks Ed. If you hadn't come along we would have had to let Wally go. But he's been here so long, nobody wants to be the guy who fires him. This Six Sigma thing could be just the ticket."

Then proceed to build up the Lost Soul by telling him or her that the Black Belt job is a piece of cake, and that you know that, with all his/her experience (eight positions over the last six years) it will be a breeze. The LS will love the training, as it means they are temporarily off the hook to actually deliver results. They won't bother to actually lead the project team, and probably won't do any work at all, unless pushed by their manager. Even then, they won't know what to do or whom to ask for advice. Likely as not, this Black Belt will drop out of the program early, leaving the project hanging. You're doing the company a favor!

Favorite quote from a lost soul: "If I don't finish this project I'll lose my job. I'm only two years from retirement. Can't you just say I did it?"

A final word about Black Belt selection: If you want the program to fail, give these jobs to people who are not really interested. The motivated Black Belt is one who *wants* to be successful in that job. Give the assignment to people who consider it a side track to their *real* career, and watch how quickly their projects come to a crashing halt.

The Master Black Belts

There is a special opportunity here to screw things up royally, even after Six Sigma has taken root in the organization. No doubt some of the Black Belts will succeed anyway, despite your best efforts to prevent this (see above section). When this happens, there will be a push to elevate these successful BB's to "Master Black Belt" status. It seems logical to move people up the ladder this way, so go along with this. In fact, take an active role and *push* people up that ladder if you have to. Here's why.

The Master Black Belt role is different from that of the normal BB. For one thing, the MBB is expected to teach new BB's and GB's who are new to Six Sigma. To be successful, the MBB must have good teaching skills. These skills are not the same as those that make a successful Black Belt, which are those of a problem solver. The MBB must also be able to coach Black and Green Belts, manage the assignment of projects, report progress to top management and so on. In other words, it is a rare Black Belt, perhaps one in twenty, who possesses the skills and desire to go on to fill the role of Master Black Belt.

Now think of the wonderful chaos when you push forward one of your Black Belts who has done a good job running his own projects, but has none of the skills required to be an effective MBB. It's rather like taking the successful flight attendant and asking him to be the pilot on the next flight. He might be happy about the promotion, but you may not want to be on standby for that flight.

Not all high performing individuals make good managers, and that's what a Master Black Belt must be.

The Financial Analyst

Do you really need this person at all? Can't the Black Belt or Project Champion do their own calculations of process savings? The beauty of this is that they will either overstate or understate the savings. If they overstate them, they erode the integrity of Six Sigma. If they understate savings, people see Six Sigma as another management boondoggle that can't pay for its own lunch.

If you must appoint a financial analyst, chose the FA using the same general guidelines as for Black Belts, above. Avoid giving them more than the bare minimum indication of what exactly they are supposed to do. Blur the distinction between "hard" and "soft" savings. Try to dissuade them from assigning Six Sigma improvements to an actual budget line. To really create a guaranteed pitfall, give this job to the most overworked accountant on your staff. They will be sure to spread the word about what a drag Six Sigma is. Stress the FA's to meet the company's targets for hard savings from DMAIC projects, and they will begin double-counting, stealing money here, hiding costs there. Eventually their activities will come to light, to the ultimate discredit of the entire program.

So, there you have it. Making sure that Six Sigma fails is as easy as giving the key assignments to the people you know will fail, and you can have a lot of fun at the same time!

The people you pick to implement Six Sigma are absolutely critical to the success of the program. The ideal Six Sigma Black Belt, for example, has a balance of statistical competence and people skills. They must have the personal drive it takes to push a DMAIC project to completion, and they need to be able to influence and persuade people at *different levels to cooperate in a timely manner. They need the courage to take chances, the discipline to follow the methodology, and the patience to deal with people who are not their direct reports. Great communication skills are a must for a Black Belt. Finally, the person you select must **want** to be a Black Belt!*

To insure success you want the best people in your company to be applying for the Black Belt positions. This means you have to actively recruit them, adequately reward them, and generously praise their results.

Black Belts must be leaders, not followers.

Okay we are going to hit the door on the count of three...
1, 2, 3!

Hmm. This Six Sigma thing IS having an impact on our organization.

Chapter 3

Communication—You announced Six Sigma once—now forget it!

Here's a real sleeper of an idea, and it requires absolutely no effort on your part! That's right, zero effort! Don't you love it already?

So, you've made your big speech in front of the whole company where you announced how you were adopting Six Sigma as your organization's path to high quality, cost savings and customer satisfaction. There was applause, nods of approval, even a few sycophants who came up to you later and asked to be considered to be Black Belts, Deployment Champions—whatever. There was a ton of enthusiasm, curiosity, and good will in the air. The field was plowed and the seeds planted. All you have to do is sit back and watch Six Sigma grow, right?

Wrong! Wrong, wrong! Wrongeddy-wrong-wrong!

The thing is, for Six Sigma to take root and flourish, it needs the fertilizer of constant communication. If you fail to say anything else about the subject, it will die off quicker than those goldfish you win at a carnival.

You see, people in an organization are always aware of what the Boss (you) wants and expects his people to do—that is, if he tells them. If you walk into the office and say, "How come we don't have lamps on the desks?" By noon, there will be catalogs in front of you, vendors lined up in the hall, and three purchase requisitions for desk lamps. That's just the way it is. People want to please the Boss.

But say you make that comment, and then later say, "Well, maybe there's enough light from the overhead fixtures." Desk lamps will not be mentioned again, except maybe by those poor folks over in the other building who never get the news until it's too late.

So, when you first announce Six Sigma, well, watch out for the river of enthusiasm that comes flowing down the hallway to your office door. People have read about Six Sigma, or heard about it from friends who work for Six Sigma companies. They see this as an incredibly forward-looking step and are excited about the opportunity it means for your company. Now, you don't want this Six Sigma thing to take over, so when they arrive at your office with their ideas, you say—Nothing!

Let's say John from production knocks on your office door (always open, of course; you are a progressive manager) and says, "Boss, I've been doing some reading about Six Sigma and I have some ideas about how we can implement this in production. I believe we can improve quality *and* cut costs."

You reply, but you don't answer his question. You say something like, "Johnny, this is the third warmest January on record, did you know that?" And if John waits expectantly for you to link this statement to Six Sigma, follow up with, "Of course, it's ruining business for the ski areas. They can't even make snow at night. Not cold enough. You a skier, Johnny?"

John may be confused, which is fine, or a skier, in which case a conversation on skiing will follow. Either way, you have taken Six Sigma off the table. Do the same to the next seven or eight people who come into your office, and Six Sigma will truly become yesterday's news.

If you are even more eager to deflate the Six Sigma balloon, simply indicate to your secretary that you are too busy with the quarterly planning to talk to anyone right now. Keep this up for days. By the end of the week, and residual support for Six Sigma will have been replaced by an overall corporate anxiety over the quarterly plan, whatever that is.

You see? You didn't have to do anything, really.

Now, let's take the case where Six Sigma has been forced upon you and there it is, and it seems to have a life of its own. Consultants have come out of the woodwork, and while you were working on the quarterly plan or something, Black Belts have sprung up and are running projects. What do you do?

Have no fear. Again, the basic 'do nothing' approach is best. If a Black Belt figured out how to cut costs in marketing by half a million, say nothing. If a team of Green Belts in quality assurance have found a way to reduce down time by ten percent, say nothing. If a brilliant engineer in the design group demonstrated how to cut product development time in half, say—what now?—that's right. You get the idea. *Nothing!*

Why does this work? Because people seem to need something called *recognition.* When they've done a good job, they expect an enthusiastic "attaboy" and a hearty handshake. Some surveys have suggested that people actually want this recognition thing more than rewards! I know you are shaking your head now, but it's true. People would rather have a few sincere words of thanks than a raise in pay.

Try a little experiment sometime. Take two of your people who are both performing OK. Tell one of them that you are absolutely delighted with their performance, and that you want to give them a special award at the next company-wide meeting. The award itself could be printed out on your secretary's computer, or give them a special parking place, maybe even a nicer cubicle (but maybe that's going too far towards a reward).

Now give the other person a thousand dollar bonus, but make them promise not to tell anybody. Just send them an e-mail and that's the end of it. Don't say thank you, and don't announce it publicly. No hand shake. What do you observe?

A week later, the first person is telling everyone how great it is to work for this company, and they have gone from being a mediocre employee to being a high performer, and it didn't cost you a dime. Meanwhile, the person you gave the thousand dollars to gives you sad, inquisitive looks in the hallway, always waiting for the handshake that never comes. He's demotivated, wondering what the heck he did wrong.

So whatever you do, do NOT acknowledge Six Sigma success in any form. It's a simple rule. You can do it.

Your clever lack of communication on the subject (i.e., saying nothing) is one of the best ways to put Six Sigma at the bottom of everyone's priority list. Here are some other tips:

- At management meetings, leave Six Sigma off the agenda.
- If some well-meaning underling sneaks in onto the agenda, tell them there's no time at today's meeting; maybe next month.
- If one of your managers wants you to hear a presentation from their Black Belt about a successful project she's just concluded, tell her, "E-mail me the presentation. I'll read it on the plane."
- If the consultant asks you to make an introductory speech for a new class of Green Belts, delegate it to your legal counsel.
- If the head of HR wants to talk to you about 'succession planning for Black Belts' or some such nonsense, say "Are we still doing Black Belts? Don't they have regular jobs to do?"

See how easy it is? You don't have to make speeches about Six Sigma, or go to classes, or ask for articles for the newsletter, or put up Six Sigma posters, or attend conferences, or network with executives in other companies with Six Sigma programs. Any of these actions might show your support for the program, and unwanted success could result.

Communication is vital to any effective corporate initiative, and it's especially true for Six Sigma. Merely announcing the program does nothing towards making it happen. All managers in the company need to be reminded that Six Sigma is not only high priority, but also that it is from now on part of the regular business of the organization.

*Assuming you really **don't** want Six Sigma to fail, it should be on the agenda of every management meeting. Take every opportunity to refer to Six Sigma when talking to small groups of employees. Let them know how Six Sigma is now a critical component of the company's success plan. Take time to personally write articles for the newsletter, or maybe even start a new publication that focuses on Six Sigma exclusively.*

Most of all, celebrate successes, no matter how small. Welcome people back after Black Belt training. Show up at a team meeting to show that you care about it. When a project is closed, make a big deal about it, even if the savings is small. A framed certificate on the wall goes a long way to building employee morale and commitment. Make the presentation of these awards public events.

Further, communicate your desire to reward those employees who embrace Six Sigma. Work with HR to assure that a succession plan exists for the people who took the initiative to become Black Belts and Master Black Belts. Chances are that these people are far more qualified than most to be the next generation of leaders for your organization.

Here is your mission Black Belt.
Agent Q can give you everything you need... a pity he's been missing for
six months.

Chapter 4

The tools for the job:
Who needs training or coaching?

If your objective is to cripple the Six Sigma effort in your organization, one sure-fire strategy is to establish the program, and then to withhold the tools people need to make it a success.

Everyone knows that a worker needs tools: a bricklayer needs his trowel, a doctor her stethoscope, a mechanic his toolbox. When it comes to the so-called white collar jobs, people are less knowledgeable about the necessity of tools, yet tools are required. You, as a manager would be lost without a telephone, a desk, office space, filing cabinets, and these days a computer with a high-speed internet connection is a must. Perhaps you also consider a mobile phone or even a "blackberry" communication device to be necessities of your trade.

In order to make Six Sigma fail, you could easily deny your Black Belts and other Six Sigma players the computers or software they need to do their jobs, but wouldn't that be a little too obvious?

But sometimes these tools are not of the hardware variety; they are the kind you carry around in your head, the competence you have built over the years. In the case of Black Belts, Green Belts, et cetera, there has not been time as yet to build this mental competency. In order for them to do their jobs, they need training, they need a lot of training, and they need it right away.

So, to ensure the downfall of Six Sigma, postpone the onset of this training as long as possible. As a leader, you have the organizational clout to postpone things indefinitely. Schedule a number of planning meetings, weeks apart. When these are finished, have a series of "infrastructure" meetings. Insist that the groundwork must be one hundred percent in place before the training can begin. With skill, you can stretch this period into months, during which time all enthusiasm for Six Sigma will evaporate.

Chances are you already agreed to pay for the bare minimum of Black Belt training, but is this enough? We doubt it. A newly trained Black Belt is like a student driver behind the wheel of a Ferrari: Can she drive it? Yes. Are accidents and/or speeding tickets avoidable? Not bloody likely.

Think about this: The Six Sigma Deployment Champion comes to you with a request for additional training so that the Black Belts can become proficient in the use of statistical software, like Minitab for example. You respond: "Why heck, Ted, we already paid good money for the training. Now you're telling me they need *more* training? What's the matter, the first training didn't take? Are you telling me we paid good money for inferior training? I think not! Do we want the Board to ask us why we spent all that money and our people still can't do their jobs? Get real!" Ted will skulk away, afraid to come back and ask again. Good work!

Here's another one that happens in this game. Some bleeding heart from HR comes and says that because Black Belts are required to lead project teams, he wants to send them to some kind of 'leadership' training. This is obviously some HR mumbo-jumbo. *You* are the leader here, not some young hot-shot Black Belt. If they picked people who can't handle the work, it's their problem, not yours. Besides, this kind of training can cost real money—and then how do you measure results? How do you measure leadership? Why, you'd be pouring good money after bad.

Not allowing high-quality training for your people is a good start, but if they're motivated enough (and if the initial training was of sufficient quality,) they just might succeed anyway, and you don't want *that*!

The other thing these Six Sigma disciples will call for is something called 'coaching'. You have possibly heard of this. Perhaps you had a coach for your basketball team in High School, or more recently, maybe you got yourself a public speaking coach before you gave a big speech to your customers a couple of years ago. Anyway, what you probably realize is that this 'coaching' stuff can make a big difference in performance.

A Black Belt or Green Belt fresh out of training has about as much confidence as a cat in a room full of rocking chairs. She takes tentative steps, wondering whether she's doing the right thing, guessing at the next step, worrying about making the wrong move. What this person needs is a good coach, one who has been there, done that. A coach can help steer the BB or GB in the right direction, warn them of pitfalls, and give them the confidence they need to go forward.

Since Six Sigma is new in your organization, who does the coaching? Who is there who knows enough about the methodology to be able to give good advice? Only the consultant, that's who. At least until you have built up an internal competency level, there's nobody else qualified for this kind of work.

Now, here's your approach: First, do nothing (remember the rule from chapter three). Then, if one of these poor struggling people come to you for support you'll know what to do. Chances are that they will come and say how they would like to have one of the consultants, a Master Black Belt, probably, (Good Lord, where did they come up with these names?) to come back and spend a day "coaching" the Black Belts with their projects.

Simply say, "You know we don't have money in the budget for that. Do you have any idea what these consultants are charging us?"

If the struggling employee comes back with some annoying piece of fact, such as, "Uh, well, boss, I checked and we DO have the budget, and the charge for the consultant is not out of line, especially considering how much money we stand to save with this project . . . yadda yadda yadda . . ."

Then you must bring out the big guns. Who's the boss here, anyway? You say, "Well, dang it, coach each other! Do this without the consultant and you'll be heroes! The more management sees these consultants hanging around here the more pressure there will be to end this Six Sigma thing and the sooner the better!" This should do the trick.

The "coaching thing" (remember George H.?) is so powerful, it could put a monkey wrench (spanner, if you're a Brit,) into your plans to make six Sigma fail, so for heaven's sake, avoid any talk of coaching.

Of course, you may be in the position where one of your own people is already a certified Black Belt, or maybe they hired a Master Black Belt from outside. This is a dangerous situation, as that person could easily coach the green Black Belts and green Green Belts. The easiest solution for you is to make sure this person is immediately transferred into a very demanding management position, so that the possibility of his or her finding time to spend coaching is minimized. This is sure to demoralize those eager GB's and BB's who were counting on that person to help them through their difficult first projects. See how easy it is to sink Six Sigma?

Now what about the other key Six Sigma players? You have the Deployment Champion, the Project Champions, the Financial Analysts. Do they need training too? Well, they do if you want Six Sigma to *work*. As your agenda differs, make it clear that these assignments are treated as ancillary to the main Six Sigma activity, and make the decision that their training is not mandatory. Once again, you will have saved a bundle of money and saved time for these poor, overworked people.

Would you withhold training and development from your most promising employees? Of course not. Assuming your aim is to make Six Sigma succeed, you must give the operatives the right tools for the job. The consultant can assist you in identifying training needs in your organization and also help to deliver that training.

Green Belts, and especially Black Belts are a little bit like the early explorers. They have taken a big risk and invested a lot of time in Six Sigma because they see big possibilities, but the waters they are sailing are new and uncharted. They, like any other professionals, need coaching, sometimes a LOT of coaching, to work their way through their first projects. After that, they may need less, and ultimately they will be able to take over the coaching responsibilities for the company. Until that time, however, you will most likely need outside expertise to help them on their way.

Stephen Covey uses the analogy of the wood cutter. He has a huge amount of wood to cut, and he senses that his saw is dull, but he also feels that he lacks the time it would take to sharpen the saw. So he continues working, harder than necessary, using a dull saw. "Sharpening the Saw" is one of Covey's "Seven Habits of Highly Effective People." Training is one of the ways we sharpen the saw. It's worth the investment.

The benefits of Six Sigma are potentially enormous. Don't scrimp on getting your people the tools to do their jobs.

The Six Sigma thing is totally under control.

Chapter 5

Planning for Failure:
Let the chips fall where they may.

If you have been following us so far, you already have many weapons in your arsenal that should enable you to sink Six Sigma. But not all of these are everyone's cup of tea. These are all fairly overt and may be obvious if not carefully employed. What if you're colleagues are fairly smart (and they might be smart, appearances to the contrary,) and you want to be subtle about your subversion? Then you've got to move on to a less obvious approach, one which should be invisible to even the sharpest eyes on your management team.

Have you ever heard the maxim: "Plan the work, then work the plan"? There's wisdom in that phrase. People who don't have a plan to work from are like builders of a house without a blueprint. Sure, the various contractors know how to nail the pieces together, but eventually you will wind up with a shower stall in your dining room.

Not having a plan for success is the equivalent of having a good plan for failure. Given your goal of destroying the Six Sigma effort in your organization, one of the best things you can do is to neglect to plan for the deployment of Six Sigma right from the start.

This is easier than it sounds. Unlike the "Do Nothing" approach to communication, this one works even if you are outwardly the biggest rah-rah cheerleader for Six Sigma in the company. You simply have to avoid, put off, procrastinate, and otherwise ignore the need for an implementation plan. People involved in the program will be so busy trying to make it happen, they won't have time to ask what the plan *is*.

Sure, questions may arise. Questions like, "how should we select projects to work on?" or "how many Green Belts do we need?" or even "how are we doing?" are more or less unanswerable unless there's a plan. If your people come to you with these questions, respond with "What do you think?" or "How do you think we're doing." Let these people state their opinions as you look like you are sincerely pondering their input, then say, "We'll do what we need to, no more, no less." This may convince them that you actually have a *secret plan* of your own.

What if your own boss is pushing you to develop this plan? Well, we suggest you resort to the most powerful tool in the manager's toolbox: Delegate. Find one of your already-overworked people in a weak moment and tell them, "Wanda, I think you're the right person to put together a plan for this Six Sigma thing. I need it on my desk by tomorrow. Any problem?" (Asking if it's any problem is optional). Of course it's a problem—but it's no longer *your* problem, and that's the important thing. If Wanda comes later to ask questions, tell her, "Wanda, I gave you this assignment because I thought you could handle it. Was I wrong?" This should cause Wanda to stand up straighter and say, "Er, no, boss, I can do it. You can count on me!" Nobody likes to admit when they are out of their depth.

And where is this fancy plan supposed to come from anyway? You've never implemented Six Sigma before. You don't want to take credit for killing the thing, you just want it to go away. Let's go back to our friend George H. Bush. It's that "vision thing" all over again. What is needed for a plan is a vision of the desired end state. It's like asking the question, "What does DONE look like?" If you know what the vision is, you can almost always work out a plan to get there, assuming you have the resources to do the work in between. No vision equals no plan, or at least a guaranteed *bad* plan.

Here's another good trick. Let's say that you're really pinned down, and you must come up with a plan, and there's no one to delegate to. Go ahead and announce a department-wide (or company-wide, or division-wide, depending on your situation,) meeting where you will announce the plan for implementation of Six Sigma. At this meeting, have slogans and banners about Six Sigma. Hand out tee shirts with your company's Six Sigma logo. Introduce all the Black Belt

Candidates, consultants, etc. Then announce the plan. Have somebody turn on the projector and there the plan is proudly displayed:

Dimbulb Enterprises, LLC

Six Sigma Implementation Plan
- $80 Million in Hard Savings
- Reduce Lead Time by 60%
- Improve Customer Satisfaction by 50%
- Reduce Waste and Rework by 70%

Isn't this a great plan? You can be proud of this plan! Management will love this plan. It has solid, measurable, "stretch" goals. It's exactly the kind of future vision the management books tell you to have. What a plan!

Except for one little thing: **_This ain't a plan at all._** The above slide is merely a collection of *objectives*. Now, while a plan is not complete without objectives, the objectives themselves don't make a plan. Calling this a plan is like calling the following a movie script:

"They kiss and walk off into the sunset."

It's like "planning" a vacation by saying: "Let's go to the Grand Canyon. We'll do some photography, take the burro ride down into the canyon, and shoot the rapids." Sounds great! Just one thing; How the heck are you going to get yourself, your spouse, three kids and a golden retriever to the Grand Canyon? Are you driving, flying, taking the train? Which route will you take? Where will you stay? When is this trip going to be, and who's going to look in on Grandma while you're away? You see, unless you're Chevy Chase, you need a bit more planning to make the objectives achievable.

But since your *real* objective is to demolish Six Sigma, just putting the objectives out there is more than enough of a plan. While the nay-sayers and nervous nellies will grouse about your "plan," other, more optimistic types will rally to the cause. People will come out of the woodwork with ideas for reaching the goals. Acknowledge these but don't adopt their suggestions, as these may be worthwhile. Charts will appear showing progress toward the "plan" goals.

About halfway through the year, people may be so distracted that they have forgotten all about the "plan". Some, however, may start to get nervous about the objectives around the time of their mid-year performance review. Your tactic here is to remind them of the plan, and tell them that you expect the objectives to be achieved come hell or high water! This should instill some real panic around the end of the third quarter, and utter devastation by the end of the year.

Now, suppose you work for a company where the management is somewhat more sophisticated than this (we doubt it, but it's possible). Perhaps they, your boss or the management team, are asking for a serious plan, consisting not only of objectives, but including a timetable, process map, organization chart, budget, resource allocation scheme, etc.? What then? If you do all that, you just might make it possible for Six Sigma to succeed! Yikes!

Don't panic. Instead, give them what they want. That's right, give them the plan, only make sure you lock yourself in your office and *write the plan yourself*. That's right, yourself. Chances are you will come up with a nice, professional-looking plan with all the necessary bells and whistles. The management team will be impressed, and you can go back to playing Minesweeper secure in the confidence that *it will never work*.

What's that you say? It won't work? But I wrote it myself!!!

Relax. We're not saying you don't know how to write a plan; whether you do or not is immaterial. The fact is that if you work in a vacuum, without input or feedback from other involved stakeholders, then you will have indeed created a plan for failure. This is not a reflection on your planning prowess, it's just a fact of life. Unless people participate in the planning process, they feel no need to take the plan very seriously. You can bet your laser printer that you will be deluged with e-mails all through the next week pointing to glaring problems with *your* plan.

With *your* plan in place, people will be faced with conflicts of resources, personnel, schedules and objectives. When it comes down to the crunch at the end of the year, you might catch some flack, like, "We couldn't meet the Six Sigma goals in our department because Ed's plan didn't allow for the seasonal surge in phone activity and didn't take into account the current hiring freeze." This is OK too, as you couldn't be expected to know all these things in advance, could you?

Oh, and if you do have a plan, please remember the lesson of chapter 3: Don't tell anyone that the plan exists.

So, in conclusion, if you absolutely must make a plan, make sure you do it by yourself with no other input. Of course, no plan at all is the best plan for failure.

If, on the other hand, you want to make Six Sigma work in your company, a plan for implementation is absolutely essential. This should be done right from the beginning. To make this plan, assemble a team from all the affected departments and make sure that everyone's view is heard. This team should get some introductory training on what Six Sigma is all about. Learn from the experience of other companies, but take the culture of your own organization into account. Your consultant can help you with all of this, but the finished plan must be "owned" by everyone.

There need to be simple, "SMART" objectives stated and agreed to up front, and these goals should be supported by a clear strategy for attaining them. At the next level should be an action plan that lists specific activities, assigns each responsibility to an individual, and states a time for completion. Once agreed, this plan must be clearly communicated to the entire organization at a meeting arranged for that purpose. There's nothing wrong with slogans and tee shirts, as long as they don't detract from the main message, which is: We are planning for the success of Six Sigma, Here's how it affects YOU.

Follow up on the objectives at every management meeting. Tweak the plan where necessary but don't abandon it if you encounter obstacles. Identify specific roadblocks, and come up with rational solutions for each. Publicize progress made toward the objectives and celebrate successes. Plan the work and work the plan!

Now you can get off the hook if things get scary.

Chapter 6

Letting Middle Management off the hook

Let's talk for a while about the people who really run this world. I'm not talking about the politicians or the army or the big bankers. I'm not talking about CEO's or Boards of Directors. I'm talking about middle managers in companies like yours. Oh, the big shot executives and directors might call the shots, but the middle managers are the people who decide where those shots will fall, for better or for worse.

In some organizations, the lucky ones, the middle managers are perfectly aligned with the top guy (or gal). In those outfits, everything that needs to happen actually gets done. In many organizations, maybe in more than you think, it doesn't work that way. It's not that the middle managers are outwardly hostile or opposed to the CEO. It's much more subtle than that; it's possibly even unconscious.

In at least one major company, the lower level managers refer to a certain middle management resistance to change as "the Layer of Clay." Whatever the CEO expresses or wants never manages to trickle down past his direct reports, or the people who report to them. As one astute expert put it, a CEO with great ideas who lacks the support of his middle managers is about "as useful as a chocolate teapot."

It works like this. The CEO makes his/her wishes known by communicating to the whole organization in very general terms, and makes a statement like, "Six Sigma is the way of the future for Amalgamated Underwear, and we will make Six Sigma a reality in our organization by 2008." Everyone hears the same message, reinforced by e-broadcast messages, posters in the halls, and lapel pins for all employees in the shape of boxer shorts with the logo "6σ in '08" embossed in gold.

Not only has the CEO made a big PR splash, his/her vision has actually captured the imagination of many of the employees. They also envision the new way of thinking, the exciting power that this new approach will deliver. They might also see interesting new jobs and career opportunities opening up for them. There's a kind of optimistic buzz in the air. People are talking around the coffee station, and while there are the usual cynics, the majority of the buzz is positive.

While the reaction of the rank and file is overwhelmingly positive, others in the company are less sanguine. Who are these people? Why, it's the middle managers.

Now, it's not that the middle managers are cynical. They are not bitter, or negative, or "out to get" Six Sigma. It's just that the middle managers, due possibly to the very seniority and experience that got them their important positions, are the people who have seen things like this many, many times before. They have seen corporate initiatives come and go. They have come in different guises over the years, and bore different names; names like Total Quality Management, ISO 9000, Quality Function Deployment, Activity Based Management, Kaizen, Lean Production and a myriad of others. Some of these had their lasting impact on the company's culture in small ways, but the majority have flared brilliantly and briefly like beautiful fireworks, before plummeting back to earth, scorching a few with their hot ashes.

Who can blame the middle managers for being somewhat skeptical about this new initiative. It doesn't matter that they love their jobs, are loyal to the company and think the CEO is a fine person. What matters to the middle manager is that he has a job to do. It's a huge job, with many critical decisions to be made, many deadlines to be met, many difficult problems to overcome, and many individual employees to keep motivated, productive and happy. What the middle manager doesn't need is a new thing to worry about: something that will lay claims on his attention, stretch his resources beyond their limits and trouble his mind even more than it already is.

Into this situation, you find yourself, and your hidden agenda to make this new initiative fail. You attended the same meetings they did. You saw the looks of expectant optimism on the faces of the rank-and-file folks, and you noticed, with your careful sideways glances, the even, noncommittal gaze of the middle managers. Then you broke a little smile of your own, because you at once visualize your path to success, or rather failure.

When you finally manage a meeting with the middle manager, (which is not easy, given the fact that he works eleven hours a day already,) he will probably have many questions about Six Sigma. Among them will be the question about his personal involvement. How much time should he expect to spend, for example, selecting projects for the Black Belts and Green Belts? How much effort does he, personally, need to put into the roll-out effort? How visible does he need to be in talking about Six Sigma with his organization?

When the middle manager raises these very valid questions, you know it is your opportunity to drive a stake into the heart of the program. Simply answer him or her by saying, "Actually, Gene, you don't have to do anything really. Just let me take care of it." Gene might come back and ask you whether this is the best course of action, but chances are he or she will not. After all, the MM is trying to cut down on his/her workload, not add to it. Your willingness to lift this dreaded additional burden will be seen as a great act of kindness, a favor in fact, that he will one day be happy to return.

If the MM does push further (again, this is unlikely,) try saying something like, "Look, I'm trying to help you here. You don't want to have to worry about this new thing, do you? Oh, by the way, I've been meaning to ask you, do you take route 80 in the morning? Cause the traffic lately has been horrendous. Maybe you know a better way . . . ?" This will change the subject quickly, as all commuters believe that they have been very clever in optimizing their commuting time in the morning.

Letting the middle managers off the hook is a brilliant strategy for failure. It ingratiates you with the MM's themselves. It makes you look like a hero because you are absorbing all the burden they thought they would have to bear. Even the CEO is happy because it centralizes the accountability for the program. Of course, it does place you in the line of fire when the thing starts spinning out of control.

And it will. Department heads will start pulling people out of Green Belt training. Project team meetings will be postponed or cancelled as urgent business needs are assigned higher priority. Black Belts will be diverted from their projects back into their former responsibilities for increasing periods of time. Eventually, the projects will start to founder, and you can lean back in your desk chair. Mission Accomplished!

Now, the middle managers in Human Resources are a special case. Remember, they had a special role in the selection of the wrong Black Belts. Now, they can have a further negative role by neglecting to take any action on behalf of Six Sigma. When the HR people are hunting high and low for capable people to fill critical positions, *don't* remind them that the Black Belts are among the best-trained and most effective people in the company. *Don't* remind them that they made a special commitment to create a career path for the Black Belts in order to recruit the finest people for these key positions, and *don't* remind the HR managers that the Black Belts have a contract (written or implied, depending on your company's approach,) that assures them well-paid, challenging jobs when their Black Belt assignments are over. When the word gets out that the Black Belts are ignored or go back to the same old jobs upon finishing their Black Belt stints, well that will be the end of anybody volunteering, ever again.

But what about the backlash? Didn't the CEO hold you personally responsible for the program? Sure, but how can you be held responsible when the middle managers themselves aren't holding up their end? Besides, the CEO is worried about things like sales, stock prices and health insurance cost. He's probably not paying a lot of attention, and you're not going to try to change that, are you? If at some point the CEO calls you into his or her office and asks you, "Whatever happened with Six Sigma. How's it going?"

Just say, "Well, it's going a little slower than I would have hoped. People are really focused on their work. They'll do whatever it takes to get the job done, but it's been tough getting started. By the way, I've been meaning to ask you, do you take route 80 into work in the morning . . ."

The middle managers are the key stakeholders in any Six Sigma implementation process. They must be brought on board at an early stage and shown exactly how Six Sigma will benefit them and their departments. You must try to get their "buy-in" before proceeding with the program, and you must obtain their commitment to meet the demands of the program. Give them a realistic assessment of the time and energy involved, and also the benefits to be realized when Six Sigma succeeds. As knowledgeable managers, they will understand the potential of Six Sigma, and will want to make it work.

Keep the middle managers accountable. Require regular reports from each department on the status of implementation. Have a Six Sigma status review as a regular part of all management team meetings. Ask questions of the managers themselves so they feel a need to know what's going on in their own organizations. Simple graphic reporting such as a bar graph showing the status of each department and a green or red "health indicator" is one simple way to go. But you don't want to embarrass the MM's either. Instead, work with them. Be visible and keep Six Sigma alive in their business consciousness. Let them know that the success or failure of Six Sigma depends on their support and involvement, and that they are accountable for both.

Finally, the middle managers residing in the Human Resources function have a special responsibility for Six Sigma. In addition to assisting in the recruitment of the best people for each of the key Six Sigma positions, HR must also help create and maintain a career path for Black Belts and Master Black Belts. This is necessary if these positions are to remain high-profile, sought-after posts in the organization.

When I first walked in here I said " Oh cool! Office pet" and he said " No it's our Business Model!"

Chapter 7

Keeping people in their "Silos"
—fight cross-functionalism

The following strategy for sinking Six Sigma is a little more subtle, so please pay attention. The beauty of it is that you can employ this method even if Six Sigma is not your primary responsibility! Why let the Six Sigma guys get all that credit?

This idea is based on the fact that you have a distinct job to perform. In order to accomplish this job, you are given people and a budget for which you must fight tooth and nail every twelve months, given today's infatuation with things like "downsizing" and "streamlining". You know you will be held to certain objectives upon which are based your bonus and your career. The last thing you need is a bunch of other work and responsibility. Practically every manager in your organization is faced with the same set of constraints.[*]

With this background, along comes the CEO and some fancy consultant who try to convince you that Six Sigma is the answer to your prayers. Using their much-ballyhooed ideas, the company will supposedly save millions. What will they do with all this savings? Will they give you more people? More money? Don't make us laugh.

What you will no doubt observe about these Six Sigma people is that they will insist upon looking at things from a "process" point of view. The processes

---

[*]   Except Human Resources, who are accountMable to no one.

they are talking about will include things you do in your operation, but also lap over into the other parts of the company. Let's say for example, they are looking at the process for shipping an order. This process looks something like this:

1. The order department call center receives a call or e-mail from a customer.
2. The order is logged into your ordering system, which is run by the IT department.
3. One copy of the order goes to the fulfillment center, the other to accounting.
4. Fulfillment locates the goods in the warehouse, and prepares the shipment.
5. Accounting approves the customer's credit and sends an e-mail authorizing shipment.
6. The goods are shipped.
7. An invoice is sent to the customer by accounting.
8. Customer relations calls or e-mails the customer to verify that the shipment was received in good condition.
9. The customer replies that the goods were damaged.
10. The claims department is called in, and a technical rep. is dispatched.
11. An invoice is sent to the customer by central billing, with a copy to receiving.
12. After 15 days, receiving sends a dunning letter to the customer.
13. After 60 days, the case is referred to the legal department
14. Etc.

In other words, at least ten different departments are involved, all for a single, stupid order. You can see where all this is going. Into this organized chaos comes a Black Belt with some talk about reducing distribution costs. You know that damage claims are a fact of life, and besides, your friendly transportation supplier sent you a wonderful gift basket for the holidays, so why cause trouble? The system works. Why fix what ain't broke?

But OK, you don't want to be looked upon as not supporting Six Sigma, so you go along. You might even send a couple of your people to Green Belt training, whatever that is.

Then this hot-shot Black Belt calls and asks you to appoint one of your people to work with the Black Belt on her "project team." Now this is getting annoying. You have just enough people to answer the phones as it is. You can't really spare people to do this extra job, and you tell the Black Belt so. She argues that the process being "improved" is actually a "cross-functional" process, and for Six Sigma to work, she must have representatives from all the affected departments.

Simply denying the Black Belt the assistance she needs is no good. Eventually you will get a call from some higher-level manager, maybe even your own VP, telling you that you have to cooperate. Hmm, you think to yourself, this is going to require some ingenuity.

Fear not! The following guidelines for busting up the Black Belt's project have all been used and are proven effective!

Your first move is to appoint a person to represent you on the project team. Now here is an important point to note: Under no circumstances are you to attend one of these team meetings personally! If you attend, you might get sucked into this project and find yourself doing the work, and maybe getting blamed when the project ultimately fails. Keep a low profile! Instead nominate Marv to represent your department.

The Black Belt will send you an e-mail, or maybe even come to your office, to say that she really wanted Dorothy to be on this team. Stick to your guns. Dorothy is the brightest person on your staff. Tell the Black Belt that you can't possibly spare Dorothy, and that you are confident that Marv will do fine. Assure her that Marv is your hand-picked person who is uniquely qualified to assist in this project. Don't tell her that Marv is a borderline employee who was put on notice during his performance review that he has six months to get his act together or he's dead meat. Don't tell her that Marv comes in every day at nine-thirty and leaves at four, and that's only on days when he's not calling in sick. And for Pete's sake don't tell the Black Belt that Marv is the one person in your entire group that you would be happy to see take an early retirement package.

After the Black Belt reluctantly agrees to accept Marv as a team member, call Marv into your office at four o'clock (assuming you can find him). Tell Marv that he has this new assignment, and he is to cooperate fully with the Black Belt. He is to attend the meetings when he has time, but under no circumstances is he to release information, provide data, or make commitments on your behalf.

(Another approach is to not talk about the commitment part. More on that later). If Marv has questions, just tell him that the Black Belt will explain everything.

Knowing Marv, he will most likely see this as yet another imposition upon his time, and will once again start typing up his resume (but not before nine-thirty tomorrow). If not, he might actually see this new assignment as a nice distraction from his normal, boring job. That's fine, as long as he doesn't take it too seriously.

At the team meetings, the Black Belt will start asking questions abut the process, maybe trying to develop a "process map" or some kind of "cause-and-effect" analysis. You can relax knowing that Marv is on the job. Marv has no idea how the process works, so even his marginal input to the team will be worthless. Perhaps he will tell the Black Belt that he doesn't know the answer to her questions, and that he will have to review the questions with you and get back to the team with the answers at a later date. When Marv comes to you for the answers, tell him: "Look, Marv, I gave you this assignment because I thought it would be an opportunity to show what you can do. Instead you are coming back and reverse-delegating the work to me. I can't do this for you. You're just going to have to do it yourself."

This should be enough to really slow down the process. Eventually, the team and the Black Belt will realize that Marv is not really a serious contributor to the team's work, so they will stop asking him questions and essentially just work around him. If Marv is supposed to produce data, your confidence in his incompetence will be justified as he fumbles and procrastinates. If the Black Belt is worth her salt, she may have to go elsewhere for the data. All of this frustrates the process and causes massive delays.

If things get out of hand, and the project team moves forward to the "Improve" phase, don't worry. At this point, Marv will either commit your department's resources for a pilot program or a designed experiment, or, following your instructions, he won't. Either way, forbid others in your department from doing work that helps the team. Remind them that their work involves total concentration, and not to be distracted by doing the work of other departments.

You yourself may have to work hard to avoid cooperating with managers from other departments. If one of your peers calls you to ask for your cooperation, tell him, "Steve, I'm up to my eyebrows with problems with shipping (or order taking, or invoicing, or whatever it is you do). Let me worry about MY job, and you take care of YOURS. OK, Steve? Your numbers weren't the greatest last quarter, as I recall." This should serve to remind Steve that he's playing with the big boys, and that he has no right to get involved with your part of the process. *Protect your turf!*

Remember, any changes to the process that affect your operation will require YOUR approval. And who knows your business better that you yourself? Are you going to let some whipper-snapper Black Belt tell you how to run it? If Marv, poor, pathetic Marv, comes back to you with suggestions, don't be cruel. Just thank him for a job well done. Ignore the recommendations.

In the worst case, the Black Belt, or the Project Champion, or worse yet, the VP, will come back to you and tell you to implement the changes that the team has decided. They will tell you, "You had Marv on the team, and Marv said that these changes could be made with no trouble."

Your response should be, "Marv had no authority to commit to any changes." If they persist, say, "I can't commit to these changes either. I'll have to do a study of the process myself and let you know what I can do later." This "study" of yours can take months—if you get around to it at all—and even then you don't have to accept the team's recommendations.

In an extreme case we know of, the department head was ordered by the CEO to make the changes. The Black Belt beamed with victory. Three months later, the changes still had not been made. When the Black Belt reluctantly reminded the department head of the CEO's order, he replied, "He's on his way out anyway. Didn't you hear?" Sure enough, the CEO retired shortly thereafter. The department head was off the hook, and the project team was disbanded, their recommendations lost forever.

What can help you in your effort to squelch Six Sigma and protect your turf is to make a series of small improvements yourself, without waiting for the team's recommendations. This will frustrate the Black Belt and send her "back to the drawing board." This phenomenon has been documented and is known as the Hawthorn Effect:

The Hawthorn Effect:

Once people start to examine a process, the process
starts to improve.

The authors have seen this many times, as managers scramble to change their operation to avoid being embarrassed by the Black Belt and her team. We have even observed a related phenomenon:

Friberg's Corollary to the Hawthorn Effect:

The manager will claim that the improvements
would have taken place anyway.

So you see, you are off the hook. The DMAIC team shrugs their shoulders as the air is let out of their balloon. The Black Belt spends a lot of time talking to herself and calling friends to find out about other jobs they might know about. You point to the improvements at a management meeting and listen as your VP praises you for your initiative.

Score: You, *1*: Six Sigma, *ziltch*.

Never mind that the Black Belt might very well have come up with improvements many times more effective than yours, and that they would have been, proven, documented and quality controlled. Never mind that your machinations will have cost the company valuable resources and time as the project team was spinning their wheels. And don't worry about the Black Belt. She's young, and will regain her confidence some day, albeit at some other company.

Least of all, don't worry about Marv. He's history.

Six Sigma does its work by focusing on processes. These processes, whether they are manufacturing or business processes, probably involve more than one single part of the organization. With the exception of the most basic of procedures, processes are cross-functional in nature, and need to be examined by people who understand these processes because they work with them on a daily basis.

The Black Belt, Master Black Belt or Green Belt is trained to look at processes this way, by utilizing the resources and knowledge of a project team. They are not trained to be superheroes working alone and in a vacuum. If your goal is to make Six Sigma successful, all involved managers need to know that their cooperation is a necessity. The people chosen for project team work should be intimately knowledgeable about their part of the process. The responsible manager must be coached to provide people he or she is sure can do this important work. After all, the manager will have to live with the team's findings and recommendations.

Team members must be empowered by the manager to act on his or her behalf, to answer questions, provide data, and work in a collaborative way with the other team members. A team charter, signed off by the affected managers, should state the overall goals of the team and fully endorse the participation of the employees selected. Rewards for completed projects should recognize all the team's members, not just the Black Belt/Green Belt.

It is part of the team leader's job to recognize when team members are not fully participating, or when the manager of a team member is being less than supportive of the team's work. The Project Champion and the process owner should then be enlisted in a corrective action to get the project back on track before too much time is wasted.

Finally, "Hawthorn Effect" improvements are fine, but they do not constitute a replacement for the team's work. If these improvements are sound, they need to be verified, documented, and locked in place with a Quality Control Plan. If they prove unsound, the team's work should continue according to the normal DMAIC discipline.

Bubbles you're a genius! You can type faster by hitting
more keys with a boulder ... Albert take note. Now if only
he'd wear pants...

Chapter 8

Selecting the Wrong Consultant

This goes back to the very beginning of the whole Six Sigma process, when your organization made the decision to adopt Six Sigma. Perhaps you were asked to get involved in the search for a suitable consultant to get you started. Now, what criteria do you apply in evaluating the many different consultants out there?

You could look at how much experience each consultant has in the area of Six Sigma; are they focused on Six Sigma or is it merely a side business for them? Is each consultant willing to work with your management team to tailor their services to fit the requirements of your organization? Can they provide the depth of talent needed to meet your needs? Of course, another concern will no doubt be—how much will this consultant cost us?

This last criterion is important. Naturally, companies would be negligent or even incompetent if they didn't consider cost when selecting suppliers of any kind. But, given your personal objective of making Six Sigma fail, cost can be a valuable ally. How can the choice of consultant help you attain your goal?

A wise man once told me, "Pay people peanuts and you'll get monkeys to work for you." In other words, change the above criteria around and make the cost of the consultant your paramount consideration. This will guarantee that the people you get to support your organization's Six Sigma effort will be the *least* that money can buy!

And there's another big benefit. When you come up with a consultant for half the price your management expected to pay, you'll be a hero! What better way to launch Six Sigma than to show a big savings on day one? Why, people will be calling you to tell you how proud they are to know you. A big promotion is no doubt just around the corner.

But wait a minute, after Six Sigma does fail, won't they point fingers at you? Won't you have to take the fall for this fiasco? Heck no! You simply point your finger at the bargain basement consultant and tell your bosses how they have not lived up to their contractual obligation, and that you recommend firing them. You'll be a bloomin' hero all over again! Management loves it when consultants get fired. If there are two things top management loves, it's hiring consultants and firing them.

Now, perhaps you had less control over the choice of consultant than you wanted. All is not lost. You can still make a competent consultant look like a loser by cleverly manipulating them. Here are some quick tips:

1. Downsize and downgrade the program. When the consultant tells you that you need to appoint a Deployment Champion from the ranks of senior management, make sure the person comes from the middle management ranks or lower. If they want this champion to report to the CEO, have them report to the HR manager. When the consultant tells you that Black Belt training takes four weeks, tell them that your people are so smart you're sure it can be done in two weeks, and refuse to pay for more. If the consultant says that Project Champion training is a three day course, explain that these people can't commit to more than one day of training at most, and that half a day would be much better (this one really works!). Whatever the consultant suggests, push back for a quicker, cheaper solution. What you get in return will be something like Six Sigma, but in a weakened state; kind of a vaccine *against* Six Sigma. Call it Semi Sigma, and perhaps you will end up with three sigma quality.

2. Push the consultant to build your company's program into a non-standard Six Sigma format, kind of a "Bizarro" Six Sigma*. Insist on changing the names of key parts of the process, and change them to negative-sounding monikers if possible. So instead of DMAIC, for example, tell them you

---

* Superman and Seinfeld fans will know what we mean here. Ask one of them for an explanation.

want to call it "DEMONIC": Define, Explain, Measure, Optimize, Noodle over, Improve, Control. Or, you might try "DEMEAN" (figure out your own acronym), which in itself communicates your low expectations of Six Sigma. Call the Green Belts something else. Ignore Black Belt certification requirements. If you are truly brave, drop the Six Sigma designation altogether, and replace it with something clever and classy like "Quality Under All Circumstances" (QUAC) or "Capability And Productivity Standardization for Quality And Total Customer Happiness" (CAPSQUATCH). Making these changes will make it impossible to use standard Six Sigma materials, and the consultants will waste plenty of time trying to bend, twist and fold their material into a new shape that fits your own, new vision, sort of.

3. Or, take the opposite tack and simply avoid getting involved with the consultants at all. They are there to run this program and get paid for doing so. Don't ask questions, or check to see how things are doing. You don't want it to work anyway, so who cares how it's going. (Caution, this one could blow up in your face if the consultants really *do* know what they are doing, causing an unwanted Six Sigma success story.)

4. Phase out the consultant about a year before the organization is ready for it. Tell the management team that you have made such magnificent progress that you feel that your own people can "take it from here". Do this before you have any of your own certified Master Black Belts, or preferably before any of the Black Belt projects have displayed any real hard savings.

Any of these approaches will befuddle your consultant's attempts to make Six Sigma a success and frustrate your own people who whine that they want to "do it right" or some such nonsense. Ignore these people. Remember, your goal is to have Six Sigma fail and to make yourself look good in the process. Ultimately, it's not how well the company does, it's how good YOU look, right?

Selection of the right consultant is absolutely critical to the success of Six Sigma in your organization. Don't think you can go with the cheapest solution and cross your fingers that it will work. Select a consultant based on their experience in launching Six Sigma in other companies. Ask whether they will assign certified Master Black Belts to the effort in your company. Make sure that they have sufficient depth in their own organization to support your effort.

Changing Six Sigma around or adopting some clever new name will not help. Six Sigma has won international acclaim because it works when applied in a prescribed, defined way; it works because it follows its own principles! Efforts to try to make Six Sigma fit into some company-specific mold will not only hurt the effort, it will negate chances for your own people who see a possible career as a Master Black Belt, and it will also fail to attract qualified Six Sigma personnel from outside.

Stay involved with your consultant from the beginning. Make sure that what they are doing makes sense, but don't challenge them on the "nuts and bolts" of Six Sigma. This is what you are paying them for. Your commitment with the consultant should be for the long haul, which means several years in most cases. You don't want to cut yourself loose from them while you are still at sea and beginning to founder.

Six Sigma is an incredibly strong and reliable methodology when implemented correctly. A consultant with a proven track record can help you make sure of success in your operation.

Now if you can get this done by six... that would be great!

Chapter 9

Selecting the Wrong Projects:
Setting the Black Belts up for failure

Sooner or later, the success or failure of Six Sigma in your organization will be judged on performance. Management will review the results of projects and determine whether Six Sigma has lived up to its billing in terms of reduction of defects, elimination of waste and rework, and saving money. Because Six Sigma calls for documentation of these things, it will not be easy to fool management on these points. It will all be there in nice, clear powerpoint charts: Either Six Sigma works, or it doesn't. So if your goal is to make it fail, it will be tough for you to "fake" failure; it will *really have to fail!*

Now, what can you do as a manager, aside from the tactics we've already discussed, that will make sure that these results are truly less than anticipated? Luckily for you, there is still something you can do, and that is to influence the choice of projects that the Black Belts, Master Black Belts and Green Belts are working on.

Six Sigma is pretty clear on the kind of projects that lend themselves to this methodology, and we have tried to summarize these in the following table, along with helpful hints on how to screw them up.

Six Sigma Requirement	Criteria for Suitable Project	Recommended for Failure
Problem Statement	The business problem is clearly stated	The problem statement is vague, or is not stated at all
Recurring Action	The process is repeated frequently	The process is repeated rarely or not at all
Aligned with Corporate Objectives	The project is clearly aligned with the company's business objectives	The project has little or no bearing on what is important to the company
Measurable	There are readily available data on both input and output variables	There are few or no measurable inputs or outputs, or they are hard to find
Potential for Savings	High potential for savings	Little or no potential for savings
Scope	Scoped to fit an acceptable timeframe	Scoped to make it impossible to fit any reasonable timeframe
Fit to BB's ability	Difficulty of project is a good fit with the Black Belt's level of competence	No Bloody Way can that boob finish this project.

Note that in the above chart we are focusing mainly on DMAIC type improvement projects. However, with a little creativity, the same thinking can apply effectively to Design for Six Sigma (DFSS), Lean, and Kaizen projects. Now let's take each of these requirements and talk about how each of them can be used to scuttle a project.

The Problem Statement

Sometimes a great idea for a project can be torpedoed by management simply because management refuses to take the time to think the problem through enough to even state what the problem is. After all, analysis to this depth is beyond the normal thinking range of most managers, whose minds are fully occupied with many other vital functions.

For example, let's say that you know that there has been a big problem lately with excess inventory of your figmagee product in the warehouse. You might state the problem as follows: "Current figmagee inventory levels exceed planned levels by 14%, causing aging and scrapping of older units, in addition to crowding of units on shelves." This is wrong, from a failure point of view, because it clearly states what the problem is. A much better approach would be, "Too many units in the warehouse," or even better, "Fix the inventory situation." Notice the beauty of the last example, as this is not a problem statement at all. The Black Belt will waste a lot of time figuring out things like "inventory of what? Where? What situation?" The clearer you can make the problem statement up front, the easier you make the Black Belt's job, so shoot for big-time obfuscation at this stage. Let the Black Belt figure it out. With any luck at all, the Black Belt will make a completely inappropriate interpretation, leading him into a dead-end project.

Recurring Action

DMAIC projects look at processes that are repeated many times, allowing statistical methods to be utilized. If you pick a process that is repeated very seldom, you make the project almost impossible using standard Six Sigma methods. A good example would be a project like: "Improve the quality of next year's product launch." Since, presumably, next year's product launch will occur only one time, it does not meet the recurring action criteria. The Black Belt will spend lots of time wondering how to get data on "next year's product launches" of the past. If he is clever, he may search the records for examples of defects from previous product launches in hopes of identifying potential failure modes, and conduct a failure mode effects analysis (FMEA) as a way of preventing defects in the future event. However, if he is a truly smart Black Belt, he will refuse the project and ask for a different one.

But the average Black Belt, especially if this is his or her first Six Sigma project, will spend months cowering in his or her cubicle, hugging a security blanket, and refusing to answer the phone.

Aligned with Corporate Objectives

One way to assure that Six Sigma gets a bad name in the organization is to make sure that the projects assigned to Black Belts are not linked in any way to the critical objectives of the company. So, let's say that the company's goals are "Improve Sales, Increase Profitability, and Improve Customer

Satisfaction." A good project to assign to the Black Belt might be something like "Improve the process flow at the salad bar in the employee cafeteria." Or, "Improve the process for handling managers' monthly mileage reimbursement statements." Or how about "Reduce warranty cost by cracking down on customer abuses."

In the first two examples, it's hard to make a connection between the projects and the company's objectives. OK, there might be a very indirect connection if you accept the idea that improving the lunch line in the cafeteria will boost morale and thereby improve productivity and profitability, but it's a huge stretch to link the two. We can't see how the internal process regarding mileage statements can affect profitability or sales, unless managers are so angry with the current process that they are on the verge of attacking the accounting department.

The last one is a good example of a project that accomplishes two very negative things. First, the implication that we will reduce warranty cost by putting the screws to our customers flies directly in the face of objective number three—improve customer satisfaction. Second, this project statement violates another rule of project assignment: Don't tell the Black Belt ahead of time what the solution to the problem is (unless you want Six Sigma to fail). The authors have seen many cases where the managers seem to know in advance what the "real" solution to the problem is. If the managers already know, why do they need Six Sigma? And why haven't they already fixed the problem?

Assigning projects that don't support the company's objectives is a perfect way to trivialize the impact of Six Sigma and thereby give it a bad name among the management team. Sooner or later, someone will point out that here we have this expensive program that isn't really helping with the critical issues of the company. The CEO will be forced to agree, and divert the resources elsewhere. Mission Accomplished!

Measurable

Six Sigma depends on numbers, so find a project where there are no numbers, or no good ones, anyway. This will assure that the Black Belt spends weeks, even months, trying to track down data that doesn't exist, or exists in the most un-usable form.

An example of this could be, "Improve sales closing ratio," where the closing ratio is defined as the number of sales divided by the number of qualified customers who visit the store. This sounds simple enough, except that when the Black Belt looks into the project, she finds out that nobody has been bothering to count the number of qualified customers who visit the store. She will have to invent a measurement system, and this will need to include a way to determine what constitutes "qualified". Then she will have to start collecting data, as there is no historic data upon which to base her analysis. Months later—still no improvements. What has this Black Belt been doing with her time anyway?

Another approach is to find projects where data indeed exists, but it is so obscure or inaccessible that the Black Belt is utterly frustrated in his attempts to dislodge it. An example of this would be trying to get data from a big, national survey like the J.D. Power Customer Satisfaction Study. Everybody knows who the winner was, (not our company,) but how can we get the data from the study that will tell us about *our* customers. When the Black Belt investigates, he finds that he *can't* get this data, because the company did not subscribe to this particular survey, and that there is no money in the budget for him to subscribe now. Next year, maybe. Sorry.

Sometimes the Black Belt makes failure easy due to his own actions. Instead of making it easy by asking for a simple spreadsheet, he can insist that a customized report is needed, thereby launching a complex programming effort that takes months to complete and strains the IT budget to the breaking point. Coach your Black Belt to demand such a report.

Potential for Savings

If you want to make Six Sigma look bad, one of the easiest ways is to dream up projects so trivial that the combined cost savings won't pay for one week of Black Best Training, much less the whole program. This is not as easy as it sounds, as Black Belts tend to be smart, motivated people (unless you did what we told you in the earlier chapter about choosing the wrong people,) and they will look hard for ways of reducing cost.

The example above, about the lunch line in the employee cafeteria, is the kind of project we're looking for here. Think small, think easy. You have spent thousands of dollars training this Black Belt, and she has years of education and experience behind her. She is ready, willing and able to tackle a big project that will really help the company. Dig around and find somebody's "pet peeve" and assign that to her as her first project. Here are some ideas:

- Improve the arrangement of parking spaces in the employee lot.
- Improve the process for hiring temps.
- Update and improve the New Employee Handbook.

Now, note several common themes. All of these are focused on internal processes that affect the ultimate customer not in the least. The costs involved are probably minor (unless your process for hiring temps is to fly to Rio De Janeiro when you need one,) and they tend to be HR related. Also, the last one is not a recurring process (although updating the book might be). The important thing is that there will be no major cost savings coming out of these projects.

To get back to hard cost savings, projects don't have to be trivial to offer little opportunity for cost savings. You can have very large, meaningful projects that are successful, but result in no hard savings. Often these projects are related to improvements in customer satisfaction, where the link between customer satisfaction and cost is suspected, but not demonstrated by verifiable data. These projects are great, and your company needs a number of these to get the maximum benefit from Six Sigma. Since your job is to make Six Sigma look *bad*, why not have *all* the projects *just* look at customer satisfaction? Any cost savings from these projects will be of the soft, squishy variety, not the kind you can assign to a specific budget line. The management team will agree that these projects are "nice". You get the idea.

Project Scope

If there is one sure-fire way to sink a Black Belt's chance of success with a given project, as well as all his or her self-esteem, it is to assign them an un-doable project. You know these projects as well as I do. They have names like:

- Reduce all product defects by 90%
- Reduce customer calls by 60%
- Improve sales in the Southern Region by 50%
- Reduce pollution in the Atlantic Ocean by 20%
- Find a solution to Global Warming
- Cure World Hunger

OK, we admit that the last three might be a little beyond the realm of credibility (unless you work for the United Nations,)* but we have seen numerous projects that are more or less like the first three, no kidding.

But, you say, what's wrong with these projects? They are measurable, you have the data, they talk about recurring events, and they are aligned with corporate goals, so what's wrong? Simply put, the DMAIC process is not designed to handle such mega-processes as those described above unless they are broken down into their component parts by applying the **"Y=f(x)"** approach.

What a Black Belt is trained to do is to take something like "reduce all product defects" and perform a Y=f(x) analysis in order to identify a new set of dependent variables, or Y's, that together comprise "all product defects". From this set of Y's, the Black Belt may find one or two that contribute most of the defects. He can then "scope-down" the project into smaller chunks that can be easily handled by one or more Black Belts or Green Belts.

Now let's get back to your mission: to destroy Six Sigma. Therefore, keep the projects huge. Avoid Black Belt attempts to scope-down the assignments that you give him or her. Insist that they look at the "big picture," which is how the CEO sees it, so why shouldn't you?

The Master Black Belts or Deployment Director may come back to you and tell you that what you have assigned the Black Belt is really a "mega-project" that would require several Black Belts or Master BB's to handle properly. Use this as an opportunity to shrug your shoulders and say "I thought Six Sigma was supposed to be a powerful tool. I guess it isn't so powerful after all, huh?" If one of them hauls off and slugs you on the spot, you have an excellent case against Six Sigma right there.

---

*   Wouldn't it be interesting to apply the Six Sigma methodology to problems such as this, allow Black Belts to scope down these problems into their component parts, and tackle each "Y" until these problems are solved? This is beyond the scope of this book, but interesting to think about.

Fit to the Black Belt's Ability

You know that you need to assign three projects to three Black Belts. One of them is certified, with several successful projects under his or her belt. Another is a recently trained candidate who shows promise, and the third is a candidate whose capability you question. You have three projects with three distinct levels of difficulty, so which do you assign to each? Logic would dictate that you give the most difficult project to the most experienced person, the next hardest to the capable but inexperienced person, and so on.

However, your logic is focused on killing Six Sigma, so you apply the opposite logic—give the hardest project to the person least likely to succeed, the next one to the person of average ability, and . . . hey, wait a minute. The middle person gets the same project in both cases. What is wrong with our anti-logic here?

If you are going to succeed in your effort to destroy the program, you need to think harder (not much, just a little). Give the most difficult problem to the inexperienced but capable person. Your ineptness at coaching (see chapter 4) will assure his failure. Give the next most difficult problem to the person of marginal competence, and his failure will also be assured. Then waste the experienced Black Belt's time on the easiest problem. She will be updating her resume halfway through the project.

We believe that by now you should have many great ideas for guaranteeing failure through the poor selection of DMAIC projects. Good Luck!

All Six Sigma training and textbooks give clear guidelines about the selection and assignment of projects to Black Belts, Master Black Belts and Green Belts. If your goal is to make Six Sigma succeed, you need to make sure that all managers are fully aware of the expectations and limitations involved. Make sure that managers are not selecting vague problems or refusing to define problems adequately. Make sure that projects meet the criteria of recurring actions, measurable data, and alignment with corporate objectives. Also make sure that there is a balance between high potential cost savings and "pure" customer satisfaction focus in the project mix. Don't allow managers to suggest projects where they already have a pre-determined solution in mind.

Be on the lookout for "cure world hunger" types of projects, unless they are accompanied by a rigorous scoping-down process that results in a few manageable projects being identified. Make sure that the projects that are assigned to a specific Black Belt are within his or her range of ability: less difficult projects for candidates still in training, more difficult ones for experienced people. In all cases avoid the trivial time-wasters or projects that represent an individual manager's "pet peeve."

The most important thing you can do if you want the right projects given to the right Black Belts is to establish a process for identifying project opportunities that involves your entire management team and the Deployment Champion. By taking the company's critical business objectives and applying the Y=f(x) principle, you should find it relatively easy to identify projects that meet all the criteria for good DMAIC projects. Go to it!

Chapter 10

Forget the Customer

Why did your company decide to implement Six Sigma, anyway? Was it because it seems like a fashionable thing to do these days—some sort of magical formula, a kind of corporate voodoo to guarantee success? Was it because competitors have already seen results from the program? Or was it because your management understands the importance of Customer Satisfaction and the parallel need to eliminate waste?

Focus on the Customer (here with a capital C*) is a central tenet of Six Sigma. Without the Customer, the concept of "quality" is meaningless, because the very definition of quality depends on meeting the needs of the Customer. Six Sigma-speak talks about "CTQ's"—critical to quality, as those demands that must be met in order to satisfy the Customer. It talks about "VOC"—the voice of the Customer, as the one and only determinator of whether quality exists at all in a product or service.

What better way to obliterate Six Sigma than to ignore the Customer altogether?

Given the above explanation, you may think that this is impossible. Not so. It is in fact very easy to forget about the ultimate customer in a shower of

---

* "Customer" capitalized refers to the end customer or ultimate consumer of the product or service. The word customer in lower case may also refer to an internal customer or intermediate customer.

enthusiasm about improving things for the *internal customer*. Now, if you have already gone through TQM or ISO 9000, you have a good picture of who the internal customers are; they are the next people downstream in a process, but still within the company. So therefore, manufacturing is a customer of engineering, shipping is a customer of manufacturing, employees are customers of the maintenance department, and so on.

Is it wrong to apply Six Sigma to internal processes that have no direct impact on the ultimate Customer? Absolutely not. Some of the biggest savings can be found in these internal processes, where waste and rework are rampant. Here are some examples of internal projects with potentially big payoffs.

- Optimize warehouse inventory to reduce carrying costs
- Reduce duplication of effort in the accounting function
- Streamline the purchasing function to assure just-in-time delivery
- Improve building climate control to reduce energy costs
- Eliminate the need for end-of-line inspection

These may all be very valid projects, (assuming they meet the criteria for good projects as previously discussed,) but it is hard to see how any of them benefit the ultimate Customer, unless the cost savings are passed along.

Now let's get back to your agenda. Since Six Sigma is all about the Customer, why not discredit it by focusing only on those internal processes that have no impact whatsoever on that very important person? That's right. Keep the focus of your Six Sigma program strictly internal. Avoid those projects that talk about "improving Customer satisfaction." Make sure that the project selection process (if there is one) focuses only on internal processes, the more arcane the better.

Drive for projects that have nothing to do with removing defects that plague the Customer. Push instead for those projects that save money here and there, preferably to the possible detriment of the final product. An example of this could be a project to "improve the productivity of K line by 3 percent." This is no doubt a worthy cause, but what impact will it have on the Customer?

Your company decided to adopt Six Sigma because the leaders recognized a gap in the ability of the organization to deliver products or services that the Customer wants, and still make a sustainable profit for the shareholders.

What happens when you limit your focus to internal processes only? Without a Six Sigma quality mentality, your products will continue to underwhelm the Customer. While consumers read about your company's profitability, they will question the wisdom of purchasing low-quality goods or services when many high-quality alternatives exist. Customer loyalty will start to decline, and unless quick action is taken, sales will start to drag.

Congratulations! You have just made Six Sigma a failed concept.

The Voice of the Customer is the driving force behind any quality improvement effort. Let's not forget the Customer in our striving to eliminate waste within the organization. There needs to be a balance between projects that stress internal process improvement and those that improve Customer satisfaction.

Change?! No .. Mister Scrooge one lump of coal was quite enough.
A goose and the next thing you know Tiny Tim will be hopping
around asking for an IPOD!

Chapter 11

Resisting change: Everything has worked OK—Why change it now?

Now, Oh serious and dedicated manager, we come to the difficult crux of the entire Six Sigma movement. These Six Sigma people, these consultants and CEO's and top executives who have bought into the whole Six Sigma *thing*, They are out to do something that flies in the face of your years of experience and business knowledge. What are they trying to do? They are trying to *change* things. That's right, and we will say it again, just incase you skimmed over it the first time: *they are trying to CHANGE things!* Six Sigma is all about change. It may start in a small way with these little projects here and there, some of which are simple and quick and, you may have to admit, even helped the business in some small way. But *change?*

Why change? After all, you have been in business for years and you see no reason to really change, other than small improvements, a little fine tuning, perhaps, a little tweaking around the edges. Your company has been successful long before Six Sigma reared its ugly, statistical head. You and your management colleagues each know how to run his or her little part of the business (except for that annoying person in purchasing—you could do without him). So what is all this talk about change, and why is so important?

As The ancient Chinese warrior Sun Tzu taught his men: "Know your enemy!" The sooner you know about this secret Six Sigma agenda, the better. After all, you are reading this book because you see Six Sigma as an enemy plot, a plot that will ruin your comfortable world, perhaps shake it to its very foundations.

Six Sigma is all about change: They would change your approach to business at the most fundamental level with their "Y is a function of X" approach to business and their dedication to always listening to the "Voice of the Customer". Heck, if the customer is so all-fired important, why isn't HE running the company? But the Six Sigma advocates will tell you that everything you do must be focused on the customer, and in fact that everything you do that is not directed toward customer satisfaction is waste. *WASTE!* You must understand this point for the threat it really is.

Take your warranty department: These are decent, hard-working people whose job it is to make sure that the company's money is not wasted. If Six Sigma is overly successful, this department might be cut right down to the bone, possibly eliminated altogether. Is that right? And what about the dedicated people in the accounting department who spend their days in laborious analysis, looking for ways to find a few more dollars in receivables, locating mis-spent allocations, and making the balance sheet, well, balance. Will Six Sigma make this department redundant with its goals of eliminating defects? Will your bowling buddies be out pounding the pavement because there are no more errors, no more outstanding debt, no more bad checks?

And what about production? Will manufacturing operations be so error-free that management might start asking about whether we really need a separate quality inspection group at all? Don't laugh. If Six Sigma is successful in achieving all this change, your company's processes could be so well designed and secure that the whole idea of inspection and rework could become as antiquated as the buggy whip.

Yes, beware of change. You always had a nagging fear of change, and here it is, practically thrust upon you. Of course you hate change. Who doesn't hate change, aside from a wet baby?

Six Sigma doesn't stop there. They want to change the way you *think*, too. They want you to think of your entire operation in terms of *processes* that must be designed to be *capable*, and that there must be quality controls locked in place to assure them. Even more, they want manufacturing to be *error-proof*, so that defects and rework will be things of the past. With this kind of thinking, it won't be long before they start examining *your* department's part in all this, and figuring out how to eliminate *your* nice, tidy job!

Oh, they will say things to alleviate your fears, things like: "Don't worry Jack, the people who used to do this wasteful work can be put to good use doing more *value-adding* work for customers." Customers again; don't they ever get sick of talking about these dang *customers?*

What can save you? What can you do to resist this change? Well, luckily for you, change turns out to be a difficult thing to accomplish, and highly trained managers like you are ideally located in the company to make change extremely difficult, or even impossible. In order to defeat change, you must fight it at several levels: 1. Denial, 2. Opposition, 3. Acceptance, and 4. er, we'll talk about 4 later.

Denial

Deny that change is taking place at all. This is your first and safest bulwark against change. Simply make believe it isn't happening. When somebody says at lunch, "Gee, this Six Sigma sure is changing things," you reply, "It doesn't really change things Mitch, it's just a tool, like a computer or a torque wrench. It's a good tool, but that doesn't mean we have to change. By the way, I think the whole thing is going to blow over after the third quarter sales figures come in. Please pass the pepper."

When your management team insist that real change in the organization is possible, reassure your department employees by saying, "Now I know that all this talk of change has you all a little nervous. Rest assured that nothing here is going to change in any big way. Just go ahead and do your jobs and keep your heads down, and this too shall pass." This may cause a few raised eyebrows among the Ivy League crowd, but your steady words of assurance will serve to calm everyone down so they can get on with their daily work, unconcerned that their lives will soon be impacted by this oncoming train.

Even when the Black Belt projects start scrutinizing your little corner of the company, don't despair. Deny, deny, deny. Whatever little tweaking and fine-tuning they recommend, thank them politely and then go back to the way you always did things.

Opposition

If denial doesn't work, and you see Six Sigma beginning to have a serious impact on your company's thinking and acting, it's time to bring out the big gun: opposition. Resist change at every level. When the subject comes up at meetings, tell everyone, "I'm not going to go along with all this change without putting up a fight, believe me. Any of you who feel the same are cowards if you don't join me in resisting this thing." Having said this, you may notice the boss getting progressively redder around his neck, and your colleagues clearing their throats and sinking lower in their chairs. Don't be intimidated! You are making a stand here based on principle, your principle being that *change is bad*. It upsets the natural order of things. It threatens your way of life. Darn it, it's a communist plot!

Use all your time-proven management skills to throw a spanner (that's a monkey wrench, if you're not in the UK) into the Six Sigma machine. Re-read the previous chapters and find out where you went wrong. Undo the damage you've done by canceling Black Belt projects, reassigning Black Belts into "value-adding work," (It's great when you can throw this Six Sigma jargon right back at them!) and undo all the process improvements that have already been put into place. If, at the end of these actions, you are still working for the same company, you will have struck a blow for resistance to the status quo!

Acceptance

What if, in spite of all your hard work in opposition to Six Sigma, you find it is taking hold anyway, and all your colleagues are starting to sing the same tune? What if there is a growing core of competency in the organization, and DMAIC projects are opening and closing all the time, with surprisingly good results? What if you find that your company's processes are reaching world-class capability, and product defects and warranty cost are plummeting? You may have to lower you silhouette slightly and hunker down until Six Sigma passes, as it surely will, won't it?

There is nothing dishonorable in accepting the inevitable, when despite your best efforts, change is upon you. Learn how to grit your teeth and congratulate the Black Belts who deliver the big cost savings. Learn how to smile when, no matter how hard you tried to prevent it, customer satisfaction starts to rise. Learn how to raise your glass and join in the toast when the CEO announces that corporate profits are on the rise again, and costs are down. You'd be surprised how easy it is, once you get the hang of it.

Commitment

This is the fourth strategy for dealing with change, the one we didn't talk about before. If you get to this point, your efforts to sink Six Sigma will have failed, and there is nothing else to do but to dig in and enjoy the fruits of victory. You have lost, and now the facts are speaking for themselves. Six Sigma works. They have finally convinced you, converted you. And you better get about the business of changing *yourself*, kiddo, or you will soon find out what life is like in a different company.

But hey, maybe that's what you really want anyway. If you are that opposed to Six Sigma, perhaps you're better off in an organization where nobody has even suggested it. But you would have learned from your experience. Next time, you will be ready!

---

*Yes, Six Sigma **is** all about change, and when its philosophy is understood by all people at every level of the organization, the speed of constructive change will astound you. Yes, unnecessary positions will be lost, but if your company is smart, there will always be homes for the bright, productive workers whose jobs have to change.*

Every change in people's lives takes them through these phases of Denial, Resistance, Acceptance, and Commitment. You can't expect people to jump from zero experience with Six Sigma right into total commitment. The whole process takes time, patience and help from people who have experience in managing change. It could turn out to be a very bumpy road for your organization, and there may well be casualties along the way. But if you are committed to Six Sigma and follow the roadmap carefully, the Six Sigma philosophy will bring about enormous changes in how you look at customers, how you manage your processes, and how you eliminate wasteful work from your company.

Stick with it. Avoid the pitfalls we have tried to present in what we hope was a humorous way. Make good use of your consultant's team, and above all, have faith in your own people. If you do a good job managing the process, your people will be eager to jump aboard the Six Sigma train. It's a train that takes you to success and beyond—all the way to world-class excellence!

A Few Final Notes

We hope you had a few laughs reading this book. It's nice to have a little fun in our business lives, and we hope we have not crossed the line from satire to cynicism.

On the other hand, the things that can be done to damage the Six Sigma effort in your organization are no laughing matter. People on the management team can commit the same errors discussed in jest in these pages, and these mistakes are not usually intentional. In fact, they are often committed with the best of intentions.

As with any venture, the effective integration of Six Sigma into your organization requires constant focus and vigilance. Your management team needs to be thoroughly engaged in the process, and management at every level must be involved and educated in the Six Sigma methodology.

When selecting your Six Sigma Integration consultant, ask yourself these questions: Does the consultant have expertise and experience in your type of business? Do they offer a full range of deployment, learning, functional and project support? Can they be relied upon for such products as customized training materials, Six Sigma recruitment services, Champion workshops, and on-site project coaching? Above all, do they have the combination of performance excellence and flexibility to work effectively within your corporate culture?

Success or failure often depends on the selection of the right team to lead your effort. The team at GELRAD is uniquely qualified in this regard. As a world class Six Sigma provider, GELRAD offers a full scope of integrated services, led by certified Six Sigma Master Black Belts.

Need help? Have questions? Contact GELRAD at 1-315-292-0952 or see *www.gelrad.com.*

www.ingramcontent.com/pod-product-compliance
Lightning Source LLC
Chambersburg PA
CBHW022120170526
45157CB00004B/1702